The B.  ·6

ᘒ

The Brussels Broadcasting Corporation?

How pro-Brexit views have been
marginalised in the BBC's
news coverage

David Keighley and Andrew Jubb

CIVITAS

First Published January 2018

© Civitas 2018
55 Tufton Street
London SW1P 3QL

email: books@civitas.org.uk

ISBN 978-1-906837-94-5

Independence: Civitas: Institute for the Study of Civil Society is a registered educational charity (No. 1085494) and a company limited by guarantee (No. 04023541). Civitas is financed from a variety of private sources to avoid over-reliance on any single or small group of donors.

All the Institute's publications seek to further its objective of promoting the advancement of learning. The views expressed are those of the authors, not of the Institute.

Typeset by
Typetechnique

Printed in Great Britain by
4edge Limited, Essex

Contents

Authors

David Keighley has worked in the media for most of his career. A graduate of Emmanuel College, Cambridge, where he worked on the university newspaper, *Varsity*, he was a reporter on the *Wakefield Express* and *The Evening Gazette*, Middlesbrough. He worked for the BBC for seven years, rising to become television news and current affairs television publicity officer with responsibility for all the corporation's highest-profile programmes in that domain. He was controller of public affairs at the breakfast channel TV-am from 1985-92, where he was in charge of all aspects of the £100m company's public profile, including editorial compliance. From 1993 to the present, he has worked as a media business development consultant, and his clients have ranged from Reuters Television to Channel Nine, Australia. He was the originator and director of News World, the world's first international conference for news broadcasters, which ran from 1995-2002, and founded News-watch in 1999.

Andrew Jubb read English and Media studies at Sussex University, with a strong focus on media bias, politics and representation. He has worked for News-watch since its inception in 1999. He has overseen more than 8,000 hours of broadcast media monitoring, and conducted extended analyses of the tabloid and broadsheet press. He has co-authored the News-watch reports and has provided statistical evidence for papers published by the Centre for Policy Studies and Migration Watch.

News-watch is one of the UK's leading media monitoring organisations. It has conducted around 40 separate reports into elements of the BBC's output, including for the Centre for Policy Studies, and has acted as consultant in a number of independent media surveys. It has given evidence to the Commons European Scrutiny Committee's audit of broadcasters' EU-related coverage 2013-2015.

Foreword

This is the latest in a long series of systematic analyses of BBC coverage of the EU, which exposes its sustained bias. Many other people have drawn attention to the BBC's failure to fulfil its duty of impartiality, but none has been based on the solid research of News-watch. The typical reaction of the BBC to criticism is to be dismissive. Systematic counting of pro- or anti-EU guests on programmes has been derided as mere bean counting, usually followed by insisting that qualitative assessments give far more insight, when the BBC has no intention of carrying out qualitative assessments either. Some years ago America's CIA became notorious for its doctrine of 'plausible deniability'. The BBC uses a similar approach. It allows the occasional guest on *Today* or *Newsnight* who is an undoubted supporter of Brexit. Never mind that the balance of coverage is biased. In a world of short attention spans it's enough to say that in the last month Tim Martin and John Longworth were on the *Today* programme. And we'll ignore how interviews were conducted: kid gloves and reverential listening to Ken Clarke and Dominic Grieve, but hectoring and interruptions for EU critics.

What is the point of publishing this research? It's certainly not because anyone at the BBC will take any notice. It is run by people who are shameless. But we hope that enough members of the public will gain improved understanding and that in time improvement may follow.

This is not the first time that biased coverage has been exposed. In 2004 it was expected that there would be a referendum on the proposed EU constitution. It never happened but an inquiry into the impartiality of the BBC was established in 2004, chaired by Lord Wilson of Dinton, who as Richard Wilson had been a distinguished civil servant until 2002, ending his career as Cabinet Secretary and head of the home civil service. There were four other members of the panel, two enthusiasts for the EU and two critics. The enthusiasts were Lucy Armstrong, chief executive of The Alchemists, and Sir Stephen Wall, the former head of the European Secretariat at the Cabinet Office and a board member of Britain in Europe, a pressure group founded originally to support British membership of the euro. The critics were Rodney Leach, chairman of Business For Sterling, and Nigel Smith, the former chairman of the No (euro) campaign. Despite the presence of committed supporters of the EU project, the panel reported in January 2005 that there was substance in the widespread public concern that the BBC suffered from 'certain forms of cultural and unintentional bias':

In essence it seems to be the result of a combination of factors including an institutional mindset, a tendency to polarise and over-simplify issues, a measure of ignorance of the EU on the part of some journalists and a failure to report issues which ought to be reported, perhaps out of a belief that they are not sufficiently entertaining. Whatever the cause in particular cases, the effect is the same for the outside world and feels like bias.[1]

The panel took pains to say that the bias was not deliberate, but that it was there all the same:

We were asked whether the BBC is systematically Europhile. If systematic means deliberate, conscious bias with a directive from the top, an internal system or a conspiracy, we have not found a systematic bias. But we do think there is a serious problem. Although the BBC wishes to be impartial in its news coverage of the EU it is not succeeding. Whatever the intention, nobody thinks the outcome is impartial. There is strong disagreement about the net balance but all parties show remarkable unity in identifying the elements of the problem. Sometimes being attacked from all sides is a sign that an organisation is getting it right. That is not so here. It is a sign that the BBC is getting it wrong, and our main conclusion is that urgent action is required to put this right.[2]

The most damning evidence, however, has been presented by Robin Aitken in his book, *Can We Trust The BBC?*, published in 2007. As a BBC journalist for 25 years he had been able to see things from the inside and his account of a documentary that was broadcast on Radio 4 in February 2000 casts doubt on the claim that the BBC's bias was not deliberate.

The documentary was called 'Letters to *The Times*' and was presented by Christopher Cook. It began with the revelation by Norman Reddaway, a retired civil servant from the Foreign Office, that there had been a propaganda unit at the Foreign Office called the Information and Research Department (IRD). Its original purposes had been to combat communism, but Reddaway reported that over the two years up to our joining the EEC in 1973 the IRD had been used to manipulate public opinion in the UK. One device was to get letters published in *The Times* to give a false impression of independent public support for British membership of the EEC, but far more seriously IRD had set out actively to influence journalists.[3] Most disturbing of all, it urged the BBC to replace journalists who were seen as 'anti-European'. IRD held a series of breakfast meetings, paid for by the European Movement, a pressure group that aimed to promote European integration. The meetings were organised by Geoffrey Tucker, a committed campaigner who described the purpose of the campaign as follows:

Nobbling is the name of the game. Throughout the period of the campaign there should be day-by-day communication between the key communicators and our personnel, e.g. the Foreign and Commonwealth Office and Marshall Stewart of the *Today* programme.[4]

Tucker explained during his interview that the presenter of the *Today* programme, Jack de Manio, was seen as anti-EU and that he had set out to persuade Ian Trethowan, then the managing director of BBC network radio, to replace him:

> Jack de Manio was a presenter who was terribly anti-European and we protested privately about this and he was moved. Whether that was a coincidence or not I really don't know. ... I just said listening to him it seems this man is giving a totally unbalanced view. It would appear that there is nothing good about Europe at all. And Ian Trethowan listened and Jack de Manio was replaced[5]

Roy Hattersley, a passionate enthusiast for the EU, told the BBC reporter during the same programme that he had attended one of the IRD breakfasts. Looking back in 2000 he confirmed Tucker's account:

> We were all on the same side. We were all European propagandists. We were all fighting the European cause to the extent that some of the protagonists actually drew Ian Trethowan's attention to broadcasters who they thought had been anti-European, and asked him to do something about it. Now I was so shocked that I decided I couldn't go again, it sounds terribly prissy and I am rather ashamed of sounding so pious, but it really did shock me at the time and, frankly, remembering it now, shocks me still.[6]

When the referendum on the EU was held in 1975 the impression was given that the mainstream media were all in favour of staying in. It is obvious from the testimony of Tucker and Hattersley that this impression had been deliberately manipulated by the management of the BBC. Aitken concludes that what happened at the BBC in the early 1970s was 'a mini-purge of editorial staff' who were considered ideologically unsound on Europe.[7]

Hattersley told the BBC in 2000 that IRD had always preferred propaganda to reasoned argument:

> What we did throughout all those years, all the Europeans would say, 'let's not risk trying to make fundamental changes by telling the whole truth, let's do it through public relations rather than real proselytizing' and the IRD was always one to 'spin' the arguments rather than 'expose' the argument.[8]

Hattersley concluded that adopting this deceitful approach had worked badly for EU supporters:

> Not only was it wrong for us to deal superficially with what Europe involved but we've paid the price for it ever since because every time there's a crisis in Europe people say – with some justification – 'well we wouldn't have been part of this if we'd really known the implications'. Joining the European Community did involve significant loss of sovereignty but by telling the British people that was not involved I think the rest of the argument was prejudiced for the next 20, 30 years.[9]

The latest News-watch study shows that the BBC has not changed. It pays lip service to impartiality but acts more like a political party with a policy manifesto. The time has arrived for a full and independent inquiry into the impartiality of BBC news coverage.

David G. Green

Executive summary

For at least the past two decades, opinion polls have shown that a large minority if not a majority of voters have wanted the UK to leave the European Union. When the question was finally put in the June 2016 referendum, they voted to do just that by a margin of 52 per cent to 48 per cent. Yet the clear preference of a large section of the population for withdrawal, and the reasons for so many people taking this stance, have been continually under-represented in the news coverage of the BBC. As this paper illustrates, pro-Brexit voices have been marginalised in the BBC's coverage of EU issues for most of the past 20 years.

That this is the case is borne out by detailed analysis of BBC news output dating back to 1999. For instance, of 4,275 guests talking about the EU on BBC Radio 4's flagship *Today* programme between 2005 and 2015, only 132 (3.2 per cent) were supporters of the UK's withdrawal from the EU. This is linked to a longstanding reluctance to even probe the question of whether Britain should leave the EU. Between 2005 and 2011, a period during which UKIP secured 12 seats and third place in the European Parliament elections, only 20 questions about actually leaving the EU were posed. In the 1,073 surveyed editions of *Today* there was an average of one question on withdrawal for every 54 editions or every 153 programme hours. When opinion in favour of leaving the EU has featured, the editorial approach has – at the expense of exploring withdrawal itself – tended heavily towards discrediting and denigrating opposition to the EU as xenophobic, and to cast those who supported it as mostly incompetent and venal.

There has also been more than a tendency to present pro-withdrawal views through the prism of 'Tory splits' and thereby also to downplay the significance of left-wing euroscepticism. In 274 hours of monitored BBC coverage of EU issues between 2002 and 2017, only 14 speakers (0.2 per cent of the total) were left-wing advocates of leaving the EU. These 14 contributors delivered 1,680 words, adding up to approximately 12 minutes out of 274 hours of airtime.

By comparison, during the same period, strongly pro-EU Conservatives Ken Clarke and Michael Heseltine made between them 28 appearances with contributions totalling 11,208 words – over nine times the amount of airtime allocated to *all* left-wing withdrawalists. BBC audiences were thus made fully familiar with right-wing reasons for Remain. They were, by contrast, kept in the dark about left-wing/Labour support for leaving the EU. Core left-wing arguments against the EU – over its prohibition of state aid to protect jobs, the threat to the NHS from the TTIP agreement and the belief that the EU has evolved into a 'neoliberal marketplace' – were largely ignored.

These findings are drawn from a sequential analysis of the media monitoring reports of News-watch dating back to 1999. Since the European Parliament elections of that year it has compiled 38 mainly half-yearly reports based on 8,000 programme transcripts covering almost 300 hundred hours of EU content. It is believed to be the largest systematic media content analysis project ever undertaken.

The overview provided here is a shocking indictment of the BBC's failure to achieve impartiality, and in particular to incorporate the views of those who desired to leave the EU into its news output. Despite the referendum vote, this bias continues to the present day. Latest News-watch research, covering a month's editions of *Today* in October/November 2017, has found that of 97 interviews on EU topics, only nine – less than 10 per cent – were with firm long-term supporters of Brexit.

These findings are compounded by the fact that, despite frequent requests to the director general and the chairman of the BBC from a cross-party group of MPs concerned about BBC bias, the Corporation has been unable to provide a single programme that has examined the opportunities of Brexit.

This paper also chronicles for the first time how the BBC's response to News-watch's ongoing monitoring of its EU coverage has been overwhelmingly unreceptive. Mostly, the Corporation has refused to consider the findings at all. The only response it has ever issued, from the Editorial Standards Committee of the BBC Trust in 2007, was seriously flawed and distorted and twisted the News-watch methodology.

The BBC response's to this data demonstrates that its formal complaints procedure and its attitude towards legitimate criticism is designed to protect the Corporation rather than to achieve impartiality in this vital area of public debate. A massive overhaul is urgently required.

1

The News-watch record of BBC bias

Sequential analysis of the News-watch archive of the BBC's coverage of the EU, undertaken here for the first time, reveals a shocking saga of failure to reflect the United Kingdom's desire to leave.

The 38 News-watch surveys, encompassing 5,600 hours of BBC programming and the line-by-line analysis of 280 hours of EU-related content, span from the European parliamentary elections in 1999 to the present day. It is one of the largest media monitoring exercises ever undertaken: no university departments track BBC output on a sustained basis, and nor does the BBC itself.

During all that period, opinion polls regularly showed that the majority, or at least a large minority, of UK voters wanted to leave the EU. But their views have never been properly incorporated into BBC EU-related output.

Despite the referendum vote, this bias continues to the present day. Latest News-watch research, covering a month's editions of *Today* in October/

November 2017, has found that of 97 interviews on EU topics, only nine – less than 10 per cent – were with firm long-term supporters of Brexit. And only one, the businessman John Mills, could be classed as a left-wing 'come-outer'.

Among the most striking longer-term findings of the News-watch research are:

- A special week of programming on *Today* in 2001, purporting to examine the withdrawal perspective, had only one very brief interview about withdrawal itself with a supporter of leaving the EU.

- The *Today* programme in 2002 covered opposition to Ireland's acceptance of the Nice Treaty in the build-up to a national referendum through only one interview, with Gerry Adams.

- Of 4,275 guests talking about the EU on the *Today* programme between 2005 and 2015, only 132 (3.2 per cent) were supporters of the UK's withdrawal from the EU.

- The figures relating to withdrawal supporters also show that in a more detailed sample period between 2005 and 2011, only 20 questions about actually leaving the EU were posed. In the 1,073 surveyed editions of *Today* there was an average of one question on withdrawal for every 54 editions or every 153 programme hours, in a period when UKIP secured 12 seats and third place in the European Parliament elections.

- Between 2002 and 2017, a total of 6,882 EU-related speakers on the EU are recorded on the News-watch database. Only 14 (0.2 per cent) of the total – one in 500 – were left-wing advocates of withdrawal. The majority of these appearances were too short to explore their views in any detail.

- During the referendum campaign, despite BBC editorial guidelines requiring strict balance, BBC Radio 1 *Newsbeat* (the Corporation's leading news programme for young listeners) audiences were 1.5 times more likely to hear a Remain supporter than a Leave supporter. 238 guest speakers contributed to the various discussions on the referendum. The analysis shows that 45 per cent spoke in favour of Remain, 30 per cent in favour of Leave – the remainder were classed as neutral.

- In 2005, a special BBC One programme, How Euro are You?, cast those who wanted to leave the EU as 'Little Islanders' – similar in its negativity to a special *Newsnight* programme during the referendum campaign in 2016, when the Leave option was cast as Britain ending up like Sealand, a rusting Second World War defence platform in the North Sea.

- In The Brexit Collection – a series of programmes selected by the BBC as representative of Radio 4's post-referendum output – there were no attempts in any programme to explore the benefits of leaving the EU but, conversely, Brexit came under sustained negative attack. This was reflected in the balance of contributions and comment contained within the items. Only 23 per cent of contributors in the programmes as a whole spoke in favour of Brexit, against 58 per cent in favour of Remain and 19 per cent who gave a neutral or factual commentary.

News-watch began monitoring the BBC's coverage of the EU in 1999 in a survey of that year's European Parliament elections.

Despite majority support during that campaign for withdrawal from the EU,[1] there was only one interview on that theme, with the then 38-year old Nigel Farage, who was a spokesman for UKIP. In the exchange, John Humphrys bracketed the party with the BNP, and then suggested that leaving the EU was 'literally unthinkable' because of all the turmoil that would be created.

The analysis in this paper shows that this approach was typical of the BBC's coverage of withdrawal for all the intervening years; it has remained so even after the referendum vote in favour of leaving.

During the referendum period, of course, Leave supporters appeared in news programmes for the first time in significant numbers, but not at the levels required by the special referendum guidelines to achieve proper balance between the opposing arguments for Leave and Remain. As already noted, analysis by News-watch found that Radio 1's *Newsbeat*, BBC2's *Newsnight*, Radio 4's *World Tonight* and *The World This Weekend*, all had a substantial imbalance towards Remain.

Whenever opinion in favour of leaving the EU has featured between 1999-2016, the editorial approach was – at the expense of exploring withdrawal itself – heavily towards discrediting and denigrating opposition to the EU as xenophobic, and to cast those who supported it as mostly incompetent and venal.

Coming up to date, more recent analysis by News-watch is showing that, as Brexit negotiations unfold, the mission of BBC correspondents is to concentrate heavily on the inadequacy and incompetence of Leave supporters – allying them wherever possible with so-called 'Fake News' and, in parallel, to leave no stone unturned in projecting how damaging to British interests and impossibly complex the whole process is. Katya Adler, the BBC's Europe editor, has declared on the BBC Newswatch programme that she sees her role as 'to put across the European perspective' in the Brexit negotiations.[2]

A major question here is *why* the BBC is so steadfastly pro-EU. Alas, here, the News-watch analysis can provide no answers. Corporately the BBC holds with bull-headed obstinacy to the assertion that its coverage is 'impartial' despite the evidence amassed by News-watch. Yet – as already noted – it has never properly examined any News-watch report on the grounds that it is the wrong kind of research, or (without ever giving reasons) that it is incompetent.

The BBC never explored or imagined editorially how life outside the EU could be positive. In parallel, there has never been a programme or strand of investigation which has looked with hard-headed journalistic rigour at the negatives of EU membership and of the EU project as a whole.

Here follows, in more detail, the News-watch findings from 1999 to the present day. Each of the separate headings below refers to a News-watch survey, which can be found be found on the News-watch website in the 'Research and Reports' section.[3]

Phase One: 1999 to 2005

1999 European Parliament elections

There was a very low level of coverage of the elections on the flagship BBC news programmes, both on radio and television. Jeremy Paxman, then anchor of *Newsnight*, described the vote as an 'outbreak of narcolepsy', perhaps reflecting the editorial lack of commitment to coverage. There was little effort to go out to constituencies. The pro-euro Conservatives, who won only 1.4 per cent of the vote, received disproportionate coverage. Allied to this, there was a heavy assumption that the Conservative party was deeply split, when during the campaign there was no evidence of this. By contrast, although many Labour MPs were opposed to the UK joining the euro, this was not explored. UKIP, which won three seats with 7.7 per cent of the vote, had only one set-piece interview on any BBC programme. John Humphrys, in his questions to Nigel Farage, bracketed UKIP with the British Nationalist Party in its approach to immigration, then suggested that leaving the EU was 'literally unthinkable' because of 'all the turmoil that would be created'. UKIP was also mentioned briefly in an On the Record programme package on the minority parties as a whole, and was again linked with BNP.

May-July 2000 – the Feira EU summit

This analysis – the first focusing on the *Today* programme – found an imbalance of 87-35 in favour of pro-EU speakers; a failure to challenge Labour spokesmen over the unproven and alarmist claims that 3 million jobs would be lost if the UK did not join the euro; repeated emphasis on that claim that the 'high value of the pound' was a handicap to the UK (now, of course reversed in connection with Brexit!); and that there were no withdrawal-supporting speakers, despite the increased showing in the previous year's elections.

January-February 2001 – analysis of *Today's* special week of reports about withdrawal

This, it turned out, focused heavily on pro-EU and pro-euro speakers and gave them the most space: their theme was to outline arguments against withdrawal. Although there were a handful of appearances by supporters of leaving the EU, most were not asked about withdrawal itself. The only exception was Nigel Farage, who was able to make a few brief UKIP policy points. The exercise as a whole underlined how locked in the Westminster 'bubble' was the BBC editorial approach. There was no attempt, for example, to talk to withdrawal-supporting business people, or rank and file voters. Presenter Sue McGregor typified this narrow, negative approach as she outlined the aim of the week's programming. She said:

This week on this programme, we're taking a look at what it could mean for Britain if she withdrew completely from the European Union. Some people suggest that she should, what would that sort of isolation mean? Well, in the second of three special reports for us, Sarah Nelson this morning looks at the political reality of life for Britain on the fringes of Europe.

Denis MacShane, shortly to be made the UK's EU minister, posited that leaving the EU was 'flat earth politics' – this went unchallenged by the presenter.

The News-watch report concluded:

This (negativity towards withdrawal) was compounded by the attitudes and stance of the BBC correspondents covering this issue. Sarah Nelson, the compiler of the series of three special reports, assembled some of the main Euro-sceptic arguments, but chose not to include in her editing the views of those who actually did support withdrawal. Her writing…appeared to indicate that withdrawal was so far off the political spectrum that it was almost impossible to find those who would argue for it. For *Today* – and the BBC – the conundrum therefore remains of how to properly cover the debate about Europe. There is a substantial strand of opinion particularly outside Parliament, but also within it, that favours withdrawal…that number remains remarkably consistent. At the moment, little articulation is given to those views. On this showing, it appears that those who espouse withdrawal will have real difficulty ever achieving an effective platform on one of the nation's main arenas of political debate.

BBC Europe and Us week, February 2001

This was a series of linked programmes on radio and television designed to illustrate the UK's relationship with the EU. At its heart was 'Referendum Street' on BBC1 about how a vote about joining the euro was likely to go. Analysis showed it was a heavily-rigged exercise, the purpose of which was to show that if people were exposed to the real facts about the euro, they would vote to join. The young people's news programme Newsround carried a series of reports which were heavily pro-EU. On Radio 4, the historian David Sells re-wrote history by suggesting that Churchill wanted the UK to be part of an all-powerful European Union. A Radio 5 phone-in presented by Nicky Campbell from Ireland featured guests and contributors who were overwhelmingly pro-EU.

The report's conclusion was:

> ... only one main programme, Question Time on BBC1, was completely balanced. The remainder were skewed in one way or another (towards the EU and joining the euro) in that they did not weave into their own analysis and presentation sufficient views and information that came from the Eurosceptic perspective... the

strand lacked coherence and on a cultural level, put forward the largely uncontested view that the EU, and everything linked with it, was about delivering more choice for the UK.

General election 2001

The main EU-related issue of the election was whether the UK would join the euro. The Conservative approach was not to; Labour claimed to be committed to 'wait and see'. Coverage examined especially the Conservative Save the Pound campaign and looked for cracks and splits, especially by focusing disproportionately on disagreements between pro-EU figures such as Kenneth Clarke and those with a more anti-EU stance, such as party leader William Hague. The editorial treatment of the eurosceptic case was heavily linked with Tories and Tory splits – the result being that the real substance of the issues involved was not properly explored. There were very few attempts to pin Labour down on its approach to Europe, to examine the range of opinions within its ranks, or to explore potential contradictions in its stance, for example over the speed of joining the euro. Political editor Andrew Marr considered withdrawal to be 'damaging' to the Tories, either because Mr Hague was being pushed towards it by Lady Thatcher, or because growing support of it amongst candidates was pushing apart the careful compromise over Europe. Mr Marr also stressed 'how desperately worried' the Tories were that the UKIP withdrawal vote would damage their support.

The launch of euro notes and coins January 1-8, 2002

This was potentially an opportunity to explore the pros and cons of joining the euro and of the operation of the new currency. But BBC coverage presented a totally one-sided view of euro-enthusiasm, and an associated drive towards greater EU federalism. There was no balancing attempt to explore opinion in favour of withdrawal, and the opposition to the euro was projected as being from a deeply split Conservative party. Other findings included that the reports:

- Grossly over-exaggerated levels of enthusiasm for the new currency;

- Seriously underplayed doubts and euro-scepticism;

- Did not include enough facts and figures for the audience to make a balanced judgment about the new currency;

- Deliberately confused New Year's Eve celebrations with enthusiasm for the new currency;

- Contained vox pops which had voices favourable to the euro in a ratio of 4:1;

- Exaggerated enthusiasm for the new currency – people were rushing to cash machines because they simply needed new notes in order to buy things.

The use of vox pops breached the BBC's guidelines on balanced reporting. Of 57 such contributions, 28 expressed positive opinions about the euro, 15 had mixed or neutral views and only 14 (five from one sequence in Greece) were negative. Reporters spoke enthusiastically and uncritically about the *Ode to Joy* being played and of tens of thousands of people on the streets – as if it was to mark the launch of the euro, not New Year's Eve – and of a sense of 'excitement' over a currency that, it was said, 'would usher in a new era of closer union'. The business reporting of the event was equally as unbalanced, with eulogising comment about moves towards EU unity from figures such as Jean-Claude Trichet, governor of the Bank of France, and unqualified pleas for the UK now to join. Across all platforms, there was very little exploration of opposition in the UK to the euro.

Seville Council meeting, June 2002

This survey noted a now recurrent issue, of under-reporting of EU affairs, despite there being meaty issues linked to EU expansion on the agenda. EU matters took only 7 per cent of available programme time on *Today*, compared with 14 per cent at the equivalent Feira meeting two years previously, amounting to 'bias by omission'. A feature of the report was a detailed comparison between the BBC's EU reporting with the volume of EU coverage in the national press. Commission chairman Romano Prodi's EU reforms, said by the FT to be the 'most important in EU history', attracted days of comment and reportage in both tabloids and broadsheets. By contrast, *Today* covered the issues involved with only one interview, when a spokesman for Mr Prodi played down their significance as 'house-keeping'. The only voice of opposition on *Today* to what many saw as Prodi's continued march towards federalism was from an Icelandic businessman, who in a contribution of a few seconds, said the enlargement of the EU was 'a step too far'.

Year-long analysis of *Today* output on the EU – September 2002 to September 2003

In the first section, there was a continuing reduction in EU coverage and bias towards pro-EU speakers (36 against 19 who were clearly eurosceptic) and over- simplification to the point of inaccuracy – the Nice Treaty was routinely called by the BBC 'the enlargement treaty' when critics believed the main aim was closer and deeper union. These problems were typified in coverage of the second Irish referendum on the Nice Treaty (after an initial 'no' vote) when the only 'Euro-sceptic' voice in favour of a 'no' vote was Gerry Adams. Only 21 minutes in total – 14 in the week of the referendum itself – was devoted to the coverage of the referendum and no British politician was interviewed about it. This was bias by omission, which downplayed the importance for the EU project of the vote.

Another milestone was the EU Copenhagen summit in December, which considered the ambitious further expansion of the EU into eastern Europe, as well as the possible accession of Turkey. Though opinion in the UK was divided about this, *Today's* coverage was heavily biased towards those who favoured EU expansion.

A measure was that, of 4,192 words in Copenhagen coverage from all contributors including vox pops and other commentators, 3,473 (83 per cent) were from those in favour of the EU and its enlargement, against 599 (14 per cent) from a euro-sceptic perspective. The balance from political contributors was that 96 per cent of the words spoken by them were from pro-EU speakers and only 4 per cent from eurosceptic contributors.

The next major EU-related development during the year was a summit in June to consider the draft for the new EU Constitution, a big step towards federalism. A key issue domestically was whether a referendum would be required to ratify this change. *Today's* coverage of the build-up illustrated another recurring problem in the EU domain. Although public opinion supported the need for a referendum on the Constitution at levels of up to 84 percent, *Today* characterised this as 'axe-grinding' by the eurosceptic press. Further, only one brief interview (of the total of 67 relevant contributions) was with someone outside the political arena – and even that was immediately followed by heavily disparaging comments from a spokesperson for the Electoral Reform Society.

Wider opinion polling at this crucial point in the development of the EU showed that support for leaving the EU was at levels similar to the referendum vote itself in 2016. Yet 'withdrawal' was mentioned only briefly twice in the *Today* coverage of the new Constitution and then only obliquely.

The European Parliament elections, April-June 2004

UKIP more than doubled its vote to 2.7m, a 16.6 per cent share, and won 12 seats. On *Today*, there were three interviews with UKIP figures, but the main emphasis was to bracket the party with inefficiency, to suggest that it was 'celebrity-driven' (reflecting the involvement of former BBC presenter Robert Kilroy-Silk), and to explore alleged links with the BNP and racism. UKIP's approach to withdrawal itself was not explored. In contrast, the governing Labour party – which attracted its lowest share of a national poll since 1832 – was asked about, and allowed to put across, its strongly pro-EU stance with little challenge. Another element of coverage was that editorially, it was projected that the main impact of the rise of UKIP would be on the Conservatives; and there was no exploration of left-wing support for withdrawal.

Today **programme survey, 2004**

This was the period when discussion about the adoption of the new EU constitution was most intense. There continued to be a heavy skew towards pro-EU speakers in interviews, with roughly 50 per cent pro, 33 per cent anti, and the remainder neutral.

General election 2005

There was a very low level of coverage of EU-related matters (only 2.1 per cent of available airtime) across a range of the main news programmes, and a consequent failure to explore relevant issues. This was bias by omission at a time when decisions about the future direction of the EU were centrally on the political agenda. UKIP made only four appearances. They were not asked about their key policies related to withdrawal, but were asked about their approach to speed traps. Generally, it was assumed that the main damage of the switch towards UKIP that had been evident in the 2004 European Parliament elections would be against the Conservatives. There was a continued disproportionate focus on 'Tory splits' in its approach to the EU, but no equivalent exploration of differences of opinion in other parties about their EU policies.

How Euro Are You?

This report was focused on a special programme – accompanied with much PR hype – about British attitudes towards the EU, broadcast on BBC2 in October, 2005. At its core was an ICM poll with 100,000 responses. The aim was to answer the question of the programme title, to distinguish between, at one extreme, EU enthusiasts ('Mr and Mrs Chiantishire') and at the other, 'Mrs and Mrs Little Islanders'. The findings were that 57 per cent wanted to 'integrate fully' with other EU countries and that only 10 per cent were 'little islanders' who wanted to leave the EU. In reality, perhaps it only showed that on one side, respondents who liked visiting Italy and drinking Chianti were overt supporters of the EU; on the other that people opposed to EU membership did not want to be cast as 'little islanders'. News-watch observed:

> The chief problem was the 'How Euro Are You?' test's inability to differentiate sufficiently between 'Europe' as a continent with its rich cultural traditions, and 'Europe' as shorthand for 'European Union' – a political and economic project.

In short, this lavish programme exercise wasted considerable amounts of licence fee cash on a poll that proved nothing. It underlined that the BBC had a fundamental aim of trying to undermine opposition to the EU by linking it to the 'little Englander' approach.

Winter 2005 survey

After the election of David Cameron as Conservative Party leader, the *Today* programme continued in its coverage of the EU during the autumn, to focus disproportionately on the possibility of Tory splits, this time because of the decision by David Cameron to leave the EPP grouping in the European Parliament. There continued to be an imbalance of Europhile speakers at a level of 2:1; and, as the toughest EU budget round in a generation unfolded, not enough airtime was devoted to EU coverage. Yet again, withdrawal was pushed firmly on to the back burner, commanding only 1 per cent of airtime. There were only three interviews, and the main one, of Nigel Farage, was distinguished by James Naughtie, the interviewer, interrupting so many times that he spoke the most words in the exchange.

Phase Two: 2006 to 2015

Over the next nine years, News-watch filed six-monthly reports, each covering the three months leading to the bi-annual EU leaders' summits.

Summer 2006 survey

The period was marked by continuing controversy over moves towards the adoption of the EU Constitution and budget, the Doha trade talks, and continuing allegations of fraud in EU accounting procedures. Of the 166 speakers on EU-related issues, the ratio of pro-EU to eurosceptic or anti-EU speakers was 2:1. Among political interviewees, the ratio was 3:1. Representatives of eurosceptic opinion outside the UK scarcely figured at all. Of the EU-related material, less than half was devoted to structural EU issues. In consequence, major topics such as EU expansion, with only five substantive reports in the 16 weeks, and the Constitution (11 substantive reports and 22 mentions in total) received narrow, often biased (in the sense that the full range of opinions on the topic was hardly explored) and inadequate coverage.

Winter 2006 survey

This period was marked by controversy related to the continuing saga of the Constitution, moves towards a common EU foreign policy, and the reduction of national vetoes. Despite this, only 2.9 per cent of *Today*'s available airtime was devoted to EU affairs, among the lowest ever recorded. Only four items related to these structural changes featured in peak airtime, and key issues such as Bulgarian and Romanian accession, with associated fears about levels of immigration to the UK, were considered only very briefly. There was a continuing 2:1 favouritism towards europhile contributors, and despite the importance of the new EU Constitution, there was no discussion of it on the *Today* programme.

Summer 2007 survey

When the new EU working arrangements were adopted on June 23 – a radical change flowing from the new EU Constitution – *Today* devoted four times more coverage to the Glastonbury rock festival than to the eurosceptic case against the new procedures. Coverage of the eurosceptic perspective during the 14 weeks before the summit amounted to only seven interviews and 22 minutes of airtime even though the story was continually developing and there was mounting pressure for a referendum among both Conservative and Opposition ranks. UKIP, by now a main national conduit of views about withdrawal and further growth of EU powers, was not asked any questions at all about the revised working arrangements. Remarks by UKIP spokesmen in four appearances occupied only around five minutes out of 238 hours of programming covered by the survey.

Winter 2007 survey

This was the period in which the new EU Constitution was agreed. On the *Today* programme, only 6.8 per cent of airtime in the week of the signing was focused on the EU summit where this occurred – a much lower percentage than, for example in the equivalent week in 2004 when Tony Blair had announced there would be a referendum in the UK to ratify the new constitution (27 per cent). In the period, we found that there was a rare occurrence – a balance between europhile and eurosceptic speakers. However, analysis of the transcripts revealed that europhile advocates still spoke the majority of contributions – 45 per cent of the words against 39 per cent (the balance being coded as neutral). The withdrawal perspective was featured in only five interviews, all with UKIP. Most of them focused on issues related to UKIP itself rather than withdrawal. Sarah Montague's main thrust in raising the issue was to suggest to Nigel Farage that if the British public wanted withdrawal, they would have voted for it in general elections, and did not need a referendum because it was not important enough to them to warrant it.

Summer 2008 survey
Coverage of EU affairs shrank to only 3.3 per cent of available editorial airtime, despite there being an abundance of issues, including the Irish referendum on the new EU Constitution, and concerted efforts by the EU to change industrial policies to tackle rising CO_2 levels. Of the 123 contributors to EU coverage, only two (1.6 per cent) were in support of British withdrawal from the EU. The BBC claimed publicly

during this period (in statements by the director general Mark Thompson) that they were covering the withdrawal perspective adequately, but, in reality, this was the lowest level of coverage since 2002. A year previously, in adjudicating a complaint from Lord Pearson of Rannoch, the BBC Trust's Editorial Standards Committee ruled that *Today* had made an error in June 2007 in not including a UKIP contribution in its coverage of the European Council meeting. The committee said it was 'satisfied that the programme was fully aware of this misjudgement and that it was unlikely to be repeated in the future'. News-watch research found that they were wrong. The 'mistake' recurred in June 2008: no UKIP representative was invited onto *Today* to speak about the European Council meeting, the impact of the Irish 'no' vote, the implications of British ratification of the Lisbon Treaty, or to have their standpoint on withdrawal tested.

Winter 2008 survey

The period was marked by moves towards the formal ratification of the Lisbon treaty, the EU's reaction to the worldwide financial collapse and further restrictions on carbon dioxide emissions. There were 57 guests who were favourable to the EU, and only 25 who were negative towards it. Of the overall total of 139 EU-related speakers, only four (2.9 per cent) were clearly supporters of withdrawal, including the leader of the BNP, Nick Griffin. Nothing of their contributions was about withdrawal itself. Only four interview items dealt with the Lisbon Treaty.

Summer 2009 survey

This period covered the European Parliament elections. News-watch monitored 10 separate news programmes, including *Today* and *Newsnight*, between April 27 and June 6, the day of the poll. There was a very low level of reporting of EU affairs and of the election itself, amounting to only 3.7 per cent of relevant airtime. The Labour government's refusal to hold a referendum over the EU's new Constitution was tackled in only one interview with a government minister. Overall, the government's approach to EU policy, and that of those in favour of closer EU integration, were scrutinised only lightly. Those who advocated eurosceptic perspectives (primarily Conservatives and UKIP) were given a much tougher time in interviews. There were only two brief exchanges (each of about two minutes) about the case for withdrawal. Coverage of UKIP focused disproportionately on corruption, racism and inefficiency, including a colour piece by Europe editor Mark Mardell which suggested the party was the BNP in blazers[4] and noted that opinion in Brussels was that they were 'seriously unfunny pranksters'.

Winter 2009 survey

This period covered the selection of the first permanent president of the European Council, the ratification of the Lisbon Treaty by member states, the Irish Lisbon

Treaty referendum and the decision by David Cameron to leave the EPP group in the European Parliament. Findings included bias by omission – a very low level coverage of these weighty EU matters. Of 198 guest contributors on EU themes, only 13 were supporters of withdrawal, and only three made contributions on that subject.

Summer 2010 survey

In the seminal general election of 2010, the BBC's coverage of EU–related issues amounted to only 3.2 per cent of election coverage as a whole, across a range of the BBC's main news programmes. Neither main party leader was interviewed about EU policy; it seems that the BBC acquiesced to the main parties in accepting that the EU was not an election issue, despite rising pressure about the UK's membership and worries about related issues such as EU-facilitated immigration. Those advocating withdrawal – principally UKIP – had only 1.98 per cent of airtime, but went on to attract almost 1 million votes (3.1 per cent of the votes cast). There was disproportionate effort to portray UKIP – and with it, the withdrawal perspective – as mired in controversy and incompetence. The leaders' debates, the first to take place in a British general election, featured some discussion of EU-related policies, but generated less than 1,000 words of fragmentary comment on follow-up news programmes.

Winter 2010 survey

As the EU's economic bailout of Ireland got underway – and with the Conservative-Liberal Democrat Coalition now in power – only three genuinely eurosceptic Conservative politicians were interviewed in the 13 weeks of analysis of the *Today* programme. BBC journalists yet again disproportionately underlined alleged Conservative divisions over EU policy and, in contrast, did not explore properly the structural problems in the euro that had caused the Irish economic crisis. In parallel, only 1.9 per cent of speakers during the survey period were clearly in favour of withdrawal from the EU, and no withdrawal perspective was included in the coverage of EU budget negotiations or the Irish financial crisis. Another issue identified was that the BBC's descriptions of EU operations were inaccurate – for example, the European Commission was described as the EU's 'civil service' when its powers are much more sweeping.

Winter 2011 survey

This was during the period of the Greek economic bailout, and there was an exceptional volume of EU coverage, almost 22.5 per cent of available airtime, against the long-term average of 5.6 per cent. It was a period of intense debate about the UK's involvement in the EU, including about withdrawal, but despite this, there were only 37 contributors on *Today* (out of a total of 517) on EU topics who were genuinely eurosceptic, and they delivered only 11 per cent of the words spoken in this category, compared to 30 per cent by those who were europhile and 20 per cent of those from the Conservative party who, like David Cameron and William Hague, were critical of minor elements of the EU but did not advocate withdrawal. In the build-up to the debate about whether there should be a referendum on Britain's EU membership, there were only four interviews with firm eurosceptics who supported the 'yes' vote, and they were allotted so little time that they were unable to make their case on anything more than a very limited basis. Only one non-Conservative supporter of the need for a referendum was interviewed – for less than three minutes.

Summer 2012 survey

A newspaper poll on May 20 showed that, with major problems continuing in the Eurozone, 46 per cent of the UK population wanted to leave the EU. But only three speakers – 0.8 per cent of the total contributors on *Today* in the survey period – were supporters of withdrawal. The BBC was told by News-watch that, including these figures, of 1,073 monitored editions of News-watch since 2005, supporters of withdrawal had been asked only 20 questions about the subject – one question about withdrawal for every 54 editions (nine weeks) or every 153 programme hours. In the survey period, bias against withdrawal was compounded by failure to properly include the eurosceptic perspective, adding up to 50 instances in 18 hours of EU coverage – most of them incidental comments totalling only 1,661 words (c.12 minutes of airtime). There were only a handful of interviews with those advocating major changes in EU policy, compared to at least 20 alone on the subject of banking and fiscal union (most of them sympathetic). Only four interviews featured 'robust' Conservative eurosceptics such as Mark Reckless or Lord Lamont. As usual, there were no appearances by eurosceptic members of the Labour party. Pro-EU Labour figures who did appear, such as Chuka Umunna and Alistair Darling, made sweeping claims about the failure of EU 'austerity' policies, that they said were fuelling a growth in right-wing parties, and they claimed without challenge that at least 3 million UK jobs depended on our membership of the EU.

Winter 2012 survey

With tensions in the Eurozone over the Greek bailout subsiding, EU coverage by *Today* fell to below its long-term average. The bulk of EU reporting continued to be focused on economic issues, despite pressing structural matters such as expansion, which was strongly on the Brussels agenda, as were calls in the UK for a referendum on EU membership. The survey – during a period in which UKIP came second in the Rotherham by-election and when an Opinium poll for the Guardian found that 56 per cent of UK voters wanted to leave the EU[5] – noted the first interview of a withdrawalist (Nigel Farage) in *Today*'s prime 8.10am slot. There was also an increase in the number of withdrawal-supporting speakers, but most were not asked about withdrawal itself, and the total number of words spoken on this topic across the 14 weeks was only 781, adding up to only one per cent of the EU-related airtime. In parallel, a further problem was that the views of 'robust eurosceptics' made up only 10 per cent of the EU coverage. Only one figure in this category from the Labour party appeared – Gisela Stuart (at this stage she had not confirmed she wanted the UK to leave the EU) – but she spoke only 51 words. There was a strong tendency throughout to view anti-EU views through the prism of Conservative party splits.

Summer 2013 survey

Withdrawal from the EU was a mainstream political issue because of the firm Conservative commitment made by David Cameron on January 23 to an 'in/out' referendum after renegotiation of the EU treaties, and because of the unprecedented strong support for UKIP in the Sunderland by-election and in local council elections. *Today* devoted almost nine hours to EU affairs over 12 weeks. But only 513 words (3 minutes and 42 seconds), contained in six contributions, came from supporters of withdrawal talking about withdrawal (but not making its case.) None of the contributions was long enough to advance the case in favour of withdrawal. The only Labour figure to appear who was critical of the EU was John Mills, the Labour party donor. He argued that there should be a referendum over EU membership, and claimed he had substantial support inside and outside Parliament.

Today also failed to ask Conservative contributors about their attitude towards EU withdrawal. It was estimated during the period that at least one third of Conservative MPs had come to support withdrawal, but those who appeared were asked only about renegotiation. Coverage also focused heavily on a return – possibly to a worse level than at any point in party history – to Conservative infighting over the EU. So, *Today* continued to present euroscepticism in all its forms through the prism of 'Conservative splits'. In sharp contrast, *Today* gave those opposed to change in Britain's relationship with the EU ample time to advance their arguments, including (again) the hotly disputed europhile claim that 3.5m jobs would be lost if the UK was to leave the EU. As on numerous occasions in previous surveys, this key assertion went unchallenged by the *Today* presenter.

Winter 2013 survey

As the debate about the EU referendum continued, *Today* featured 186 speakers who spoke about EU-related themes, but there was a heavy pro-EU bias. Discounting those who were neutral, 63 were clearly pro-EU, and only 28 'anti-EU or Eurosceptic' (though the latter category was not completely 'anti' because it included those like David Cameron who advocated reform of the EU but wanted the UK to stay as a member). These 'pro-EU' guests had ample space to make their arguments and were encouraged by presenters to do so. Four contributions were highlighted which showed that, in over 1,800 words, these figures were able to make highly controversial points – such as that the UK was 'a nasty country' for wanting change in the movement of people directive – without effective challenge. *Today* continued to seriously under-represent and misrepresent the voices across the political spectrum who wanted to leave the EU. There were only eight occasions when figures known to be withdrawalists actually appeared to speak about EU-related themes. They spoke around 2,341 words, 4.3 per cent of the EU-related airtime. But sequences in which advocates of leaving the EU actually spoke directly on that theme were only around 800 words (less than five minutes of airtime, divided between four interviews). Of this, there was only one sequence in which the speaker had the opportunity to express more than one sentence on the topic. Detailed transcript analysis showed that the main points put to 'come outers' were that they were incompetent, potentially venal, and racist. No questions were put which attempted to explore the pros and cons of leaving the EU. This under-reporting of EU opinion was despite a December 1 poll by Opinium which found that only 26 percent of UK voters thought the EU 'a good thing', against 42 per cent who described it as a 'bad thing'.[6]

Summer 2014 survey

In the European Parliament elections, UKIP, the only party unequivocally in favour of withdrawal, won 26.6 percent of the votes, against 24.2 per cent for Labour and 23.1 per cent for the Conservatives. Yet in the entire campaign, no question was put to a 'come-out' politician on that theme, and the words spoken in total by clear supporters of withdrawal amounted only to a few brief phrases and sentences. No-one from the BBC asked: 'Why do you want to leave?' On *Today*, the editorial focus was disproportionately on allegations of racism linked to those who opposed EU immigration policies, together with questions about the integrity of Nigel Farage and UKIP. Mr Farage was treated more negatively than other party leaders in the key leadership interviews. Accusations put to him included that he was racist, Stalinist and simply incompetent. Nick Robinson, who interviewed the party leaders on *Today*, focused most on whether Mr Farage was racist over his attitudes towards immigration, and asked nothing about withdrawal itself. Two special features designed to bring viewers basic information about how the EU operated were misleading and heavily pro-EU. *Newsnight* broadcast an election special containing an interview with Nigel Farage and three segments of what was claimed to be essential information about how the EU operated. The exchange with Mr Farage was, as on *Today*, heavily negative towards UKIP and did not tackle adequately the withdrawal perspective. The three segments about the EU, by reporter Chris Cook, were clearly biased towards the EU, pointedly ignored or distorted the eurosceptic perspective, and over-simplified to the point of banality some of the issues involved. This was particularly striking in the description of the workings of the European Parliament.

Winter 2014 survey

In a switch of emphasis, News-watch monitored four programmes for eight weeks in the autumn and winter of 2014: *The World At One* and *PM* on Radio 4, *Newsnight* on BBC2 and *News at Ten* on BBC1. Similar problems were found as on *Today*. Coverage of the issues surrounding possible withdrawal from the EU was minimal and inadequate. Most news about Conservative handling of EU affairs was through the lens of alleged party splits, which BBC correspondents claimed had been raging since Maastricht. Effort to cover these divisions was disproportionate, and there was insufficient analysis of current policies; exploration of rows took precedence over informing audiences about the bread and butter issues of EU membership. Labour policies towards the EU were poorly covered. Party members were afforded regular platforms to attack Conservative and UKIP policies, but their own controversial approach towards limiting immigration or the potential threat posed to party support by UKIP was seldom featured or analysed. Appearances by eurosceptic Labour figures were too brief to give a true indication of the debate within the party about EU membership. There was a continued heavy focus on UKIP's alleged shortcomings, but very little coverage or analysis of key issues such as withdrawal and the limitations of the EU. And the main editorial reaction to UKIP's by-election victory at Rochester was to ask Conservative MP Philip Davies why he would not himself defect to UKIP. Another problem was that, while it was frequently said that the EU opposed reform of matters such as the free movement of peoples directive – and platforms were often given to EU figures to say that – there was no editorial effort to scrutinise why such policies could not be changed or reformed.

General election 2015 survey

Central to the poll, of course, was the promise from David Cameron of a referendum on EU membership. Despite this, the News-watch survey, covering *Today* and World at One on Radio 4, *Newsnight* on BBC2 and News at Ten on BBC1, found that only 3.1 per cent of relevant programme time was EU-related. Business coverage was particularly skewed. The focus throughout the campaign was on interviewing those who believed that leaving the EU would be damaging to business in the UK. *Today*, for example, in its dedicated business slots, interviewed only four guests who spoke in favour of the Conservative referendum policy, or who more broadly supported EU reform, against 18 speakers who said the referendum was a threat or a worry to business. None of the contributors believed that leaving the EU could benefit British business. Coverage of withdrawal was again both inadequate and viewed predominantly through the lens of racism (in relation to immigration) and problems within UKIP. There were very few appearances by Labour supporters of leaving the EU, and the party's central stance of blocking a referendum was inadequately explored.

Phase Three: The 2016 referendum

In the next stage of monitoring, News-watch scrutinised the BBC's output during the build-up to the EU referendum the following year mainly through blogs. These identified a range of significant failings, and during the campaign itself, non-adherence to the especially strict editorial guidelines. All of these can be read on the News-watch website but, for brevity, a selection of examples are summarised in the following.

Newsnight

In the build-up to the referendum in early 2016, 40 consecutive editions of *Newsnight* were monitored. A major concern was that in one-to-one interviews about the EU, there were 12 occasions (covering 14 guests), when pro-Remain guests appeared, against only six Brexit supporters. The overall imbalance in all material about the EU towards Remainers was 25-14. Other issues identified were that Kate Hoey – in a very rare appearance by a Labour supporter of Brexit – was asked not about withdrawal but perceived splits in the Leave camp; and EU figures who appeared, such as Guy Verhofstadt, were given a clear opportunity to explain why Brexit was a mistake, with no balancing material from equivalent figures who disagreed. In the formal campaign period, a series of seven referendum specials, though relatively balanced in terms of Leave and Remain guests, culminated in a panel vote of 7-1 in favour of Remain. News-watch analysis[7] showed that the likely reason was that the special programmes were deeply biased. For example, a decrepit war-time North Sea defence platform called Sealand was chosen to represent what the UK outside the EU might look like; and a programme from Boston in Lincolnshire portrayed the immigration pressures it was facing as 'extreme' and unusual, with a heavy preponderance of local and national opinion that immigration from the EU was vital for the British economy. After the vote on June 23, a strongly biased programme wrongly suggested that an Ipsos Mori opinion poll had shown that a re-run referendum would result in a Remain vote.

The World Tonight

Twenty consecutive editions of the programme were monitored in early 2016. The findings were that 19 programme guests offered pro-EU views, seven wanted Brexit or were anti-EU, and 11 were neutral. This imbalance was made worse as seven of the pro-EU figures were given the opportunity to outline detailed arguments, whereas only three of the leave figures were allowed more than one or two sentences. Three of the 20 editions went out of their way to assemble multiple comments from strongly pro-EU figures – with nothing equivalent from the Leave side. Special editions of the programme from comment about the referendum from the Costa del Sol, from the twinned cities of Freiburg in Germany and Guildford, and from Berlin were heavily biased towards Remain comment and perspectives.

The World This Weekend

News-watch analysed 15 editions in the build-up to the referendum and found that presenter Mark Mardell over-represented the Remain arguments, gave more time to Remain supporters, and featured most heavily stories which favoured the Remain side. At least seven editions were biased in this way towards Remain; none was biased in favour of Leave. A recurrent editorial approach, yet again, was the close investigation of divisions over the EU within the Conservative party. There was no equivalent exploration within Labour of issues such as the impact on the working class vote of the parliamentary party's strong support of EU immigration policies. Typical of the bias was an edition from Portugal[8] in which Mark Mardell presented a package with a heavily pro-EU emphasis. This was followed by interviews with Remain stalwart Sir Mike Rake (a past president of the CBI) and businessman Richard Tice, a prominent Leave supporter. The interview sequence inexplicably gave more than double the space to the pro-EU case.

A report from Berlin[9] was similarly biased, producing two senior industrialists, one senior politician and two students to say that Brexit would be a more or less unmitigated disaster and nightmare for the UK and would lead to the rise of nationalism and collapse of civilisation. Against this, it produced one Alternative for Germany (AfD) politician and stressed that she was from the 'hard right'.

Newsbeat

This survey was of all the editions of BBC Radio 1's *Newsbeat* (the BBC's leading news programme for young people) during the referendum period, when the programme had to adhere to the strict BBC referendum editorial guidelines. The analysis found a surprisingly low level of coverage (bias by omission), and an imbalance of guests which meant that the audience was 1.5 times more likely to hear a Remain supporter than someone from Leave. Of 38 *Newsbeat* reports with guest speakers, 19 (50 per cent) were in favour of Remain, and only five favoured Leave. There was a much greater breadth of opinion in Remain contributions – they came from Conservatives, Labour, the Liberal Democrats and the Green party. Conversely, the Leave side featured only Conservatives and UKIP. There were no Leave contributions from the Labour party or wider Left. There was no input at all from the nationalist parties in Scotland, Wales and Northern Ireland. Editorially, *Newsbeat* enhanced and amplified the view of those supporting Remain and did not subject such views and alleged related facts to due rigour. Conversely, opinions and alleged facts in favour of Leave were robustly scrutinised, made to look ignorant or contradictory, xenophobic or unfounded. In an immigration special from Wisbech, significantly more prominence was given to views favouring EU immigration, and the 'fact checking' sequence was similarly skewed about the economic contribution of EU incomers. Overall, *Newsbeat* gave biased 'fact check' assessments. It said that immigrants contribute more cash to the UK than they receive in benefits, and the impact on the UK of current levels of immigration was minimised. Opponents of current levels of immigration were cast as xenophobic and inward-looking, whereas those who approved of immigration were made to appear outward-looking, open and broad-minded.

Phase Four: Post-referendum

After the referendum, News-watch mounted a range of monitoring projects, including scrutiny of The Brexit Collection, Radio 4's selection of special programmes in the aftermath of the vote; a six-month analysis of *Today*'s business news from June 24 until December 22, the coverage by *Today* of the week in which Article 50 was invoked; a long-term study of the coverage by *Today* of Labour and 'left-wing' support for Brexit; and finally, analysis of the BBC's handling of EU content during the 2017 general election.

The Brexit Collection

This was a selection by the BBC of 24 separate programmes (and seven programme strands) on Radio 4 which discussed Brexit, mainly broadcast after June 23, but some from before the vote. Overall, there were no attempts in any programme to explore the benefits of leaving the EU, but conversely Brexit came under sustained negative attack. This was reflected in the balance of contributions and comment contained within the items. Only 23 per cent of contributors in the programmes as a whole spoke in favour of Brexit, against 58 per cent in favour of Remain and 19 per cent who gave a neutral or factual commentary. Nine programmes and six features, amounting to 5 hours 20 minutes of programming, were strongly anti-Brexit, contained unchallenged predictions that civil unrest and rioting were now on the horizon and cast the 'out' vote in negative terms, inferring that the result had been a consequence of racism and xenophobia. The balance of programme guests in all of these items was strongly – and sometimes overwhelmingly – pro-Remain. The items that were strongly anti-Brexit were editions of culture series Front Row, The Briefing Room, six editions of the feature Brexit Street on the news programme *PM*, one edition of *A Point of View, How to Make a Brexit* (a one-off documentary about Greenland's exit from the EU), *Farming Today, More or Less, The Food Programme, The Bottom Line and Call You and Yours*. In some of these, the range of anti-Brexit opinion was light years from any definition of 'impartiality' and there was no balancing comparable pro-Brexit material.

Today's business news

This extensive survey, covering from June 24 to December 22, found that the overwhelming editorial drive of business news on *Today* was to air sustained and multi-faceted pessimism about the immediate and long-term negative consequences of the vote to leave the EU. One measure was that of the 366 guest speakers, 192 (52.5 per cent) were negative about the impact of the vote and only 60 (16.3 per cent) expressed opinions which were pro-Brexit or saw the post-referendum economic outlook as positive. Only 10 (2.9 per cent) of the business news interviews (from six speakers) were with supporters of withdrawal from the EU. Between them, the negative guests painted a picture of gloom, doom and uncertainty, of plunging economic prospects, of a collapse of consumer confidence, rising inflation, a drying up of investment, job freezes, of a drain of jobs from London to mainland Europe, skills shortages because of the ending of free movement, the introduction of tariffs, and endless, complex renegotiation.

Article 50 coverage by *Today*

In the week of the filing of the UK's Article 50 letter (March 29–April 4, 2017), *Today* broadcast six editions which contained almost five hours of material about the letter and its aftermath. This was almost half of the available feature airtime – almost 10 times the long-term average devoted to EU affairs. The programme coverage was strongly biased against Brexit and made special efforts to illustrate the extent to which leaving the EU could have catastrophic consequences for the UK. There was, by contrast, only minimal effort to examine the potential benefits. A measure of this overwhelming negativity was that only eight (6.5 per cent) of the 124 speakers who appeared over the six editions were given the space to make substantive arguments that the future for the UK outside the EU would yield significant benefits. The overall gloom was buttressed by the programme's editorial approach. Presenters and correspondents, for example, pushed at every opportunity to illustrate potential (and existing) problems. At the same time, they were strongly adversarial towards Brexit supporters, but much less so to guests who advocated that the UK was, in effect, now staring down the barrel of a loaded gun. Problems that were deliberately pushed to the forefront included the wealth of the City of London being under threat, the creation of a 'legislative soup', the EU not agreeing with the UK's preferred path of negotiations, and the possibility of exit talks extending up to 10 years. BBC 'fact-checking', though presented as objective, was anything but. Chris Morris, the 'fact checker' was most focused on choosing topics that showed Brexit in a negative light, and failed at even the elementary level of pointing out that 'EU money' was actually provided by UK taxpayers.

Leave and the 'Left': 2002 to 2017

The BBC declares that it is committed to reflect 'a breadth of diversity of opinion… so that no significant strand of thought is knowingly unreflected or under-represented.' This News-watch survey found that, of 6,882 speakers on EU matters identified in 30 News-watch reports over the 15 years, only 14 (0.2 per cent) were left-wing advocates of leaving the EU. These 14 contributors delivered 1,680 words, adding up to approximately 12 minutes of airtime in 274 hours of EU coverage. One third of them came from a single 531-word Gisela Stuart appearance on *Today*, in which her actual contribution in favour of leaving the EU amounted to just 49 words. So only 1,198 words across the entire 30 surveys came from left-wing speakers making any sort of case for withdrawal, an average of 86 words per contributor. In comparison, during the same period, strongly pro-EU Conservatives Ken Clarke and Michael Heseltine made between them 28 appearances with contributions totalling 11,208 words – over nine times the amount of space allocated to *all* left-wing withdrawalists – with an average contribution length of 400 words. BBC audiences were thus made fully familiar with right-wing reasons for Remain. They were, by contrast, kept in the dark about left-wing/Labour support for leaving the EU. Core left-wing arguments against the EU were ignored, for example: the EU's prohibition of state aid to protect jobs, the threat to the NHS from the TTIP agreement, the EU's treatment of the Greek socialist government and people, unemployment in the eurozone, import tariffs for developing countries, and the belief that the EU has evolved into a 'neoliberal marketplace'. Between 2002 and 2014, there were only four left-wing contributors who supported withdrawal in the *Today* programme's EU output, adding up to just 417 words. There were more than twice as many appearances on EU matters in this period by the British National Party (BNP). In the 2015 general election campaign, despite the proposed EU referendum being a central issue, there was only one interview with a left-leaning advocate of withdrawal. During the referendum itself, there were only five contributions from Labour supporters of Brexit totalling 161 words (1 minute 31 seconds) on BBC1's News at Ten, and none at all on Radio 1's *Newsbeat*. In the Radio 4 collection of post–referendum programmes, The Brexit Collection, there were only two left-wing supporters of Brexit, and their contributions were minimal.

2

The BBC complaints procedure – unfit for purpose?

In its coverage of many subjects, it is obvious that the BBC is no longer neutral. A prime example of this is its coverage of climate change. In 2011 the then Corporation trustees declared that, because there was scientific 'consensus' on the subject, climate alarmism was justified,[1] and those opposing this should only very rarely appear on BBC programmes. Another is immigration. The Corporation's own internal 'fact check' unit has decided that the huge influx of people from the EU and around the world is of economic benefit to the UK, despite rafts of respected analysis which dispute this. And also, of course, the EU. BBC presenters and correspondents are disproportionately focused on demonstrating how massively complex the Brexit process is, and in presenting the Brussels perspective on the related negotiations. A measure of the BBC's negative approach here is that in the *Today* programme's business news coverage for six months after the EU referendum, only six of 366 guest speakers were known supporters of Brexit who made contributions on that theme.[2] At the same time, the Corporation has never presented a programme which has explored the potential benefits of leaving the EU.

In its stance on such issues, the Corporation's collective approach to the world – for whatever reasons – appears heavily skewed towards the opinions of the liberal left, with defence of the EU at the core.

The BBC, of course, denies its bias. But it is on extremely shaky ground. On the one hand are its tendentious claims about climate change. This is symptomatic of how, on a range of controversial subjects, the Corporation has adopted opinions. On the other, it simply does not permit rigorous independent assessment of its output.

Those making complaints against this overt partisanship of the BBC need a hard hat and a thick skin. It is a heavily rule-bound process, rigged in the Corporation's favour.

One immediate issue is the BBC's fundamentally skewed approach to impartiality itself. Back in 2007, the BBC trustees formally codified that, although breadth of opinion is a vital ingredient in its output, the complexity of modern debate meant that minority views – at the BBC's own discretion – should be afforded only 'due impartiality'.[3] In practice, this translates into those voices being virtually ignored. The impact was immediate in news coverage and in the reflection of this approach in other programming. Anyone who complained was told that they were wrong to be concerned; rejection of their views was justified.

The formal rules also stipulate that only complaints about individual programmes and short items broadcast in the previous 30 days can be entertained. These absurd, unduly tight restrictions preclude detailed academic analysis of programme output – of which, more later. It boils down to the fact that the whole process is designed to brush complaints under the carpet rather than to deal rigorously, openly and honestly with bias issues.

As the BBC Charter has a requirement for impartiality at its heart, this is a highly unsatisfactory approach. It is astonishing that Parliament renewed the Charter during 2015-16 without putting a more robust, independent and transparent process in place.

One change is that Ofcom, the independent media sector regulator, has replaced the BBC Trust as the final court of appeal for complaints. But what stayed exactly the same is that almost all complaints must first go to the BBC, and the fact remains that the vast bulk of submissions are dealt with by the internal BBC process, with the Corporation as its own judge and jury.

Going to appeal takes an extraordinary amount of preparation and understanding of due process. Most complainants do not have the time, resources or patience to persevere to the extent required. In turn, the entire BBC machine is attuned to finding every reason possible for turning complaints down.

A measure of the inadequacy and unfairness of the current system is that only minuscule numbers of complaints are upheld. Between April 2005 and August

2015, the BBC received 2.1 million complaints from viewers and listeners. Only 3,335 were considered to have enough substance to reach the Editorial Complaints Unit (the highest level of the internal complaints process), and of these only 12 per cent (407) were partially or fully upheld, and only 6.4 per cent fully upheld. That adds up to only one upheld every nine days – from thousands of hours of output each week by the Corporation's eight main radio and television channels and local radio network. Of course, not all of the complaints are of a high quality or soundly-based, but it is still an astonishingly high rate of rejection. The BBC adds another layer of obfuscation by publishing only limited details of its adjudications. Move along there, nothing to see.

Another aspect of complaints handling is that the BBC has two programmes which consider submissions from audiences. But both Newswatch (on television) and Feedback (BBC Radio 4) are presented by hosts who are deeply sympathetic to the BBC. They interview a succession of BBC executives and programme-makers who almost invariably trot out a variety of reasons why complainants are misguided, and contend that their submissions either ignore balancing material elsewhere, can be rejected under 'due impartiality', or are wrong.

A defence used by the BBC in its overall strategy of telling the world it is not biased is annual market research polling designed by the Corporation to find out how 'trusted' they are as a source of news. Rather predictably in a highly attenuated and fragmenting news supply and entertainment market, the BBC, as an organisation with £3.5 billion in resources and a powerful brand name used for decades, gains a high score.

But this proves nothing definite about impartiality. It is naïve and misleading of the BBC to project that the loaded questions of market research should do so. How do audiences judge? Most people dip in and dip out of coverage and see or hear only a fraction of what is actually broadcast. They do not keep track of what they hear and see, and so their responses to broadcast programming are impressionistic and reactive. It is arguable also that BBC news audiences are showing distrust by voting with their feet. *Newsnight* on BBC2, which once commanded a nightly audience of approaching 2 million, now attracts around only 500,000 and is in continuing decline.[4]

Which leads to a vital point. The only reliable and verifiable way of monitoring impartiality in the news arena is to record a range of programming over a specified period, to transcribe all the relevant material gathered, and then to use a range of rigorous analytical techniques to work out patterns and conclusions. This is partially a 'counting' exercise (in tracking, for example, the number of speakers and the volume of material) but a key component is also looking, in the context of the numbers, at the nature of individual contributions and overall editorial approach.

This is how university media studies departments throughout the world approach the assessment of broadcast media content.[5] The BBC trustees who regulated the Corporation between 2005-16 also relied on such content analysis from Cardiff and Loughborough universities, to establish that output in key areas such as the coverage of science and the use of statistics was properly impartial.[6]

Yet the senior management of the BBC news department now actively rejects such an approach. The BBC relies instead purely on its own internal judgment, carried out using methodology it has never clearly disclosed, to decide whether content is balanced. This is augmented by various senior BBC presenters who declare in press articles that they know that the Corporation's output is free from bias and properly pitched. One of the latest to do so was *Today* presenter Nick Robinson. In the Radio Times in April 2017, he invoked 'due impartiality' to rail against those who claimed that post-Brexit coverage of the EU was skewed.[7] But how he arrived at his judgment was not disclosed.

Back in 2005, a report into the BBC's EU content by a panel chaired by former cabinet secretary Lord Wilson of Dinton found that there was bias, and ignorance internally about this. His report recommended that in order to remedy the defects, rigorous internal monitoring using academic principles should be undertaken. The news department, in its formal response, agreed that this would subsequently happen.

But nothing of this internal monitoring was ever published – if, indeed, it ever took place. A decade later, in 2015, the most senior BBC editorial staff confirmed to the Commons European Scrutiny Committee that all such efforts had been abandoned because they were believed to be impractical and too expensive. They said that other unspecified and undefined internal reviews, supervised primarily by individual editors, were instead relied upon.[8]

Over the years, News-watch has attempted to engage with the BBC about the findings of its EU content surveys. It has been a highly frustrating and negative process. The Corporation has only ever formally considered one of the 38 News-watch reports. In 2006-7, while Michael Grade was BBC chairman, the Editorial Standards Committee (ESC) of the BBC Trust ordered a response to the News-watch Winter 2006 report, which monitored 84 editions of *Today* and had found there had been too few eurosceptic speakers, a poor understanding of the eurosceptic case, little exploration of the withdrawal perspective and a generally low level of coverage of EU issues, amounting to 'bias by omission'. The ESC response was an almost comical whitewash. The inquiry was conducted by a biased 'independent' adjudicator (who had been a BBC news executive for 19 years), and he used highly questionable methodology, distorted the News-watch analysis and findings, and then relied for much of his own counter-evidence on the (clearly skewed) opinions of BBC senior news personnel.[9] It was the demonstration of precisely the skewed institutional mindset which Lord Wilson's report of the previous year had warned against.

All the other reports have been formally submitted to the BBC but there has been no detailed response to any of them beyond pledges that they would be circulated internally.

Another measure of the overwhelming negativity involved in the BBC complaints process can be found in the Corporation's response to a News-watch complaint in 2013. On January 23 of that year, David Cameron announced his pledge to hold, after the next general election, a referendum on the UK's continued EU membership. That evening, *Newsnight* on BBC2 broadcast a reactive programme which featured 18 supporters of remaining in the EU and only one who wanted to leave. News-watch, backed by a cross-party group of MPs concerned about BBC bias, submitted a complaint under the BBC's formal procedure. The matter was eventually considered by the Editorial Standards Committee, but it ruled that the programme was not in breach of impartiality rules. It came to this view on the grounds that it had not been a major news event (which would be governed by special conditions of impartiality), that an edition of *Newsnight* six weeks previously had contained supporters of withdrawal, and that the aim of the January 23 programme had been simply to explore elements of the reaction to David Cameron's speech – and most at Westminster supported remain.

As in 2007, the defence amounted to preposterous stone-walling. For example, the earlier *Newsnight* edition cited by the BBC did include limited opinion in support of leaving the EU, but the programme as a whole was strongly biased in favour of Remain. There was no way it properly 'balanced' the January 23 edition. Further, the ESC's denial that Mr Cameron's speech was a major news event flew in the face of basic common sense: newspapers the following day carried dozens of pages of news reports and analysis. No appeal was allowed.[10]

The third major instance of the BBC's inept handling of matters in this arena is chronicled in *Impartiality at the BBC?*, a News-watch paper published by Civitas in 2014.[11] The background here was that in 2012 the BBC Trust commissioned television executive Stuart Prebble to investigate whether the BBC's coverage of EU affairs was properly balanced. As part of the process, the Cardiff School of Journalism was commissioned to conduct a content survey. Prebble duly gave the EU coverage a clean bill of health, but News-watch established that his conclusions were simply wrong. First, the Cardiff survey on which he relied was riddled with rudimentary methodological and sampling errors. Its claim that EU reporting was impartial was not in accord with the data. Second, Prebble also brought into his report unsubstantiated (and demonstrably wrong) 'evidence' from BBC staff, that other elements of EU content outside the Cardiff sample were properly impartial. And third, Prebble was not, as was claimed by the BBC, 'independent' in his outlook. He had close, long-standing professional ties with David Liddiment, the then BBC trustee who had appointed him to conduct the review. Prebble's subsequent approach to his task underlined that he was anything but 'independent' in the way he reached his conclusions.

Taken together, the above boils down to the fact that while the BBC, according to its Charter, must be impartial in its news coverage and programming, its approach to this is overly defensive and shot through with incompetence and conflict of interest. The primary drive seems to be to reject as many complaints as possible – to the extent of farce – and to protect the BBC at all costs. The BBC complaints procedure itself is far too narrow in what it allows to be submitted and not fit for purpose. At the same time, the Corporation's high command will not allow any other form of investigation into its output.

The one glimmer of hope as things currently stand is that Ofcom will adopt a more robust and genuinely independent approach to dealing with complaints about the BBC. But this avenue is as yet untested. A concern here is that many members of the Ofcom Content Board have worked for, or have close connections with, the BBC.[12]

Conclusion

The deluge of EU-related bias chronicled by News-watch is incontrovertible evidence of very fundamental problems in the BBC's approach to impartiality. Throughout the 18 years of monitoring, despite opinion polls showing strong and often majority support for leaving the EU, the BBC has effectively ignored the findings and carried on regardless in seriously under-reporting – and at times ignoring – the case for withdrawal. As moves towards Brexit grind forward, the fingers-in-ears approach continues, with Europe editor Katya Adler leading the charge of Corporation journalists seemingly focused on the perspective and interests of Brussels more than those in the UK who voted decisively in favour of leaving the EU.[1]

The experience of News-watch is that the BBC is obstinately determined not to consider properly its findings, and – despite promises made to Lord Wilson of Dinton – will not conduct its own equivalent research, but has nonetheless formally dismissed the News-watch evidence (without any of their own) as 'defective and loaded… (and) would not pass academic scrutiny'.[2]

News-watch would welcome an honest, robust debate by the BBC about its approach and methodology, but the BBC's only consideration of its findings was conducted – as outlined above – on a farcically rigged basis by one of its own former staff.

The BBC has been telling News-watch that it should abandon detailed academic research and stick to the rules, submitting instead complaints under the rules of the Complaints procedure – that is, on single programme items. The snag here is that when News-watch has done so, as happened with the *Newsnight* edition of January 23, 2013 outlined above, the BBC approach was also severely biased.

What all of this shows is that the Corporation is impervious to all complaints in this domain. The complaints procedure is hopelessly unfit for purpose. The one glimmer of hope is that Ofcom might adopt a different approach. Evidence of their approach from December 2017 (as this paper was being finalised) suggests not, however. It may well be that in the face of this bloody-minded intransigence, something more radical – such as a judicial review of the entire complaints process – might be the only way forward to remove this endemic, sustained, pro-EU bias.

Notes

Foreword

1   *BBC News Coverage of the European Union: Independent Panel Report*, January 2005, (Wilson report) p. 3.
2   Wilson report, p. 4.
3   Aitken, R., *Can We Trust the BBC?*, London: Continuum, 2007, p. 80.
4   In Aitken, p. 81.
5   In Aitken, p. 81.
6   In Aitken, p. 82.
7   In Aitken, p. 83.
8   In Aitken, p. 95.
9   In Aitken, p. 95.

1. The News-watch record of BBC bias

1   According to Ipsos Mori, in 1999, most voters favoured withdrawal:
    http://theconversation.com/polling-history-40-years-of-british-views-on-in-or-out-of-europe-61250
2   A transcript of the programme can be found here:
    http://isthebbcbiased.blogspot.co.uk/2017/11/its-fair-comment-to-make.html
3   This can be found here:
    http://news-watch.co.uk/monitoring-projects-and-reports/

4   The shockingly biased contribution is outlined in detail and
    put into context on the News-watch website in a blog:
    http://news-watch.co.uk/back-to-the-future-the-bbcs-attacks-
    on-eu-withdrawal/

5   Daniel Boffey and Toby Helm, '56% of Britons would vote to
    quit EU in referendum, poll finds', *The Observer*, 17 November
    2012: https://www.theguardian.com/politics/2012/nov/17/eu-
    referendum-poll

6   Toby Helm, 'Shock four-country poll reveals widening gulf
    between Britain and EU', *The Observer*, 1 December 2013:
    https://www.theguardian.com/world/2013/nov/30/shock-poll-
    reveals-gulf-britain-eu-france-germany-poland-hostile

7   David Keighley, EU Referendum Blog, 14 May 2016:
    http://news-watch.co.uk/referendum-blog-may-14/

8   News-watch, 'Mardell: Anti-Brexit bias continues', 4 May
    2016: http://news-watch.co.uk/eu-globe/

9   David Keighley, 'Mark Mardell wins Vince Cable award for
    balanced reporting as Germans warn of Brexit "nightmare"',
    30 May 2016: http://news-watch.co.uk/mark-mardell-wins-
    vince-cable-award-for-balanced-reporting-as-germans-warn-
    of-brexit-nightmare/

2. The BBC complaints procedure – unfit for purpose?

1   BBC trustee Alison Harding issued a press release in July 2011
    stating that it was 90 per cent likely that climate change was
    caused by humans and that this had moved from 'opinion to
    fact': http://www.bbc.co.uk/blogs/bbctrust/entries/a9d7d52e-
    bcf8-432d-af1f-60d82397a7fd

2   This picture is outlined in News-watch report ' The BBC
    and Brexit: Analysis of the Business News on BBC Radio 4's
    Today Programme': http://news-watch.co.uk/wp-content/
    uploads/2017/03/News-watch-Business-News-Survey-.pdf

3   This was codified and formally adopted after the BBC trustees
    commissioned a report called 'From See-Saw to Wagon Wheel'
    (a metaphor for how debate now occurs) from former BBC

producer John Bridcut: http://www.bbc.co.uk/bbctrust/news/
press_releases/2007/impartiality.html

4 Alexia James, *'Newsnight*'s Inexorable Decline', *Country Squire Magazine*, 14 December 2016: https://countrysquire.
co.uk/2016/12/14/Newsnights-inexorable-decline/

5 An overview of the approaches and complexities involved is here: https://en.wikipedia.org/wiki/Media_bias

6 The various reports can be accessed here: http://www.bbc.
co.uk/bbctrust/our_work/audiences/editorial.html

7 Sam Blewett, 'BBC "bias" in Brexit coverage defended by former political editor Nick Robinson', *The Independent*, 3 April 2017: http://www.independent.co.uk/news/media/bbc-brexit-bias-nick-robinson-defend-broadcaster-a7665316.html

8 See report of the of the committee's proceedings by Craig Byers: http://news-watch.co.uk/bbc-news-chiefs-claim-that-monitoring-for-political-bias-is-very-unhelpful/

9 A full analysis of his approach can be found at p.7 in the News-watch submission on complaints procedure reform to the Department of Culture Media and Sport: http://news-watch.co.uk/wp-content/uploads/2015/10/News-watch-submission-to-DCMS.pdf

10 The full saga can be read on the News-watch website. Details can also be found in the News-watch DCMS submission: http://news-watch.co.uk/wp-content/uploads/2015/10/News-watch-submission-to-DCMS.pdf

11 David Keighley and Andrew Jubb, 'Impartiality at the BBC?', Civitas, April 2014: http://www.civitas.org.uk/pdf/impartialityatthebbc.pdf

12 The composition in October 2016, with 10 of the 13 linked to the BBC, was chronicled here: http://news-watch.
co.uk/?s=Ofcom+

Conclusion

1   David Keighley, 'EU's Brexit "wall of silence" goes unchallenged', *The Conservative Woman*, 21 November 2017: https://www.conservativewoman.co.uk/david-keighleys-bbc-watch-eus-brexit-wall-silence-goes-unchallenged/

2   Quoted in Oliver Rudgard, 'BBC invited a third more pro-EU than Eurosceptic speakers to appear during election campaign, report claims', *The Daily Telegraph*, 22 October 2017: http://www.telegraph.co.uk/news/2017/10/22/bbc-invited-third-pro-eu-eurosceptic-speakers-appear-election/. See also News-watch's reaction: David Keighley, 'Soros attack dogs join the fray over BBC's Brexit bias', *The Conservative Woman*, 28 October 2017: https://www.conservativewoman.co.uk/david-keighleys-bbc-watch-soros-attack-dogs-join-fray-brexit-bias/